POETRY TUNED TO MY EAR

POETRY TUNED TO *my* EAR

F.M. JACKS

PALMETTO
P U B L I S H I N G
Charleston, SC
www.PalmettoPublishing.com

Copyright © 2024 by F.M. Jacks

Hardcover ISBN: 979-8-8229-4183-0
Paperback ISBN: 979-8-8229-4184-7
eBook ISBN: 979-8-8229-4185-4

Contents

An Emerging Poet

I refer to myself as an emerging poet. Writing poetry started as a therapeutic activity for me. During difficult times, my poems enabled me to cope, process my feelings, and express my truth. Eventually, poetry turned into my preferred form of creative expression.

My experiences, and those of my loved ones and friends, help me create a rich tapestry of relatable material. When I write about love, betrayal, violence, empowerment, and more, my hope is that my poems evoke reflection and conversation about the positive and negative aspects and complexities of human emotions and relationships.

In my creative process, the poems are tuned first to my own ear, but the style is similar to spoken word, a popular form of performance art. I gravitate to this style because it often involves storytelling with elements of rhyme, repetition, slang, word play, and intense imagery.

Good verse can make us feel more connected. Have you ever read a poem and recognized yourself in the experience? I invite you to read, enjoy, and reflect.

Pain

Real

Abuse takes many forms, the physical
more recognizable than others

Unsightly marks on the majestic bodies
of our daughters, sisters, mothers

Careful, do not diminish the impact on their souls

An essential part of their ability to be whole

Internal bruises culminate in a lifetime
of questionable choices

Resulting in eroded self-worth, suppressed voices

Dare I compare, but emotional abuse
takes much longer to heal

And does not make the trauma any less real

Twists and Turns

The twists and turns of a sexual deviant's mind

Foul play is the norm, and wedding vows do not bind

The cesspool of lies, too many to count

For the end game is how many bodies to mount

A place of deception and addiction

The body becomes a slave to the mind's affliction

Social media provides a means to an end

The ability to connect with many
women you call "friends"

Your boys cover for you with the trusting wife

They are accomplices to your double life

The twists and turns of a sexual deviant's mind

Foul play is the norm, and wedding vows do not bind

Your Crown

Lack of companionship makes you weary and weep

An absence of fulfillment too often lulls you to sleep

Slumber can be a form of escape—
you are depressed, numb

Challenged to face the days before they've even begun

Been in this place too long

Sedated in complacency, unsure how to move on

Can't change a person, but you can
change your circumstance

Stop telling yourself lies trying to
reimagine unrequited romance

Public opinion can create invisible chains

But to live the life you deserve you can't remain

Break through rather than break down

Don't stay in a relationship that's beneath
you—queen, claim your crown

Recognize

I gave you the best years, my youth

You gave me little consideration, no truth

Held my head high, took it on the chin

Raised to be strong, don't reveal the pain within

You relished in the deception, as if
you were playing a game

I didn't recognize my own reflection, unsure who to blame

My Desire

My desire for more pales in comparison to the
promise of what's emerging at my core

My heart beats, so I know I'm alive, but to what extent?

Longing for an authentic life directs my path

Perilous roads I navigate fuel my wrath

My heart beats, so I know I'm alive, but to what extent?

Passion evades me in a way that persuades me to be still

Fervent prayer not enough to direct my will

My heart beats, so I know I'm alive, but to what extent?

I search for a means of escape from
this relationship of woe

It isn't a matter of should or should I not go

My heart beats, so I know I'm alive, barely

I Go High

He fans the flames of discourse

Silently, I outline my steps toward divorce

While he goes low, I go high

Every word he speaks, a carefully crafted lie

Lies roll off the adulterer's tongue with little thought

No longer worrying of being caught

Assumes I would never break up the
family for the kids' sake

Motherly love won't allow me to let them share my fate

To witness such dysfunction is a lesson I'll no longer teach

Keep telling me how selfish I am—
go ahead, brotha, preach

Spinning tales as if he is the author of this story

You aren't skilled enough to pen this allegory

When he goes low, I go high

I could expose every falsehood, but why?

I have one foot out the door

This one-way argument is a bore

Money saved to plan my escape

Truly, no need for more debate

When you go low, I go high

I'm not spiraling, but you are…Why?

I never gave you permission to play
with my heart, and yet you did

You never thought I would leave, and yet a farewell I bid

Ugliness

Your ugliness is showing

Betrayal upon betrayal, counting on her never knowing

Deceitful, disrespectful when she had your back

Sneaking around with lesser women, and that's a fact

Exposed, open wide

Recounting transgressions with twisted pride

Brandishing a lethal weapon to intimidate and coerce

Stroking it like a pet during heated converse

She asked herself how she was misled by the
clandestine stranger that once shared her bed

With her out of the picture you will come to see

Your toxicity will turn inward, and the mirror will
reflect so clearly…your ugliness is showing

My Back

My back is strong, but it can't carry you

Your weight is heavy, your baggage is too

Get off my back

Please know, I won't allow your limitations
to influence how far I can go

Too long, my back up against a wall

Pressured by your insecurities, trying
to make sure you don't fall

Stop talking about having my back

You can't handle your own shit, and that's a fact

Don't pat me on the back with false
pride in my accomplishments

Your jealousy, like your approval, lost power
over me—keep that sentiment

My back is bent but unbroken

It has endured pain and represents a strength unspoken

My back marred but unapologetically on display

A visual embodiment of my life up
until the moment I walk away

Struggle

It's a struggle to co-parent with you

Serving your needs is paramount in all that you do

You have children to help raise

Yet your output is minimal, and you expect undue praise

Often absent when they need you most

About all their accomplishments you brag and boast

It's a struggle to co-parent with you

The excuses too many, the contributions too few

You give so little but expect great return

Demand so much from children for
whom you've shown little concern

Front and center at life events posturing
and poking out your chest

Astonished because we know the time you didn't invest

I struggle for my children, and for
my children I tolerate you

Real talk, I can't wait to put you in my rearview

Anxiety

I sometimes see problems where there are none

Stems from trauma when I was young

Overly cautious, fearful of the unknown

As I age, my rhythm of anxiety and
worrisome nature have grown

Intellectually I know better

Emotionally I'm unable to get it together

Aware that life will pass me by if I don't face my fears

Been wrestling with this demon of anxiety for many years

What if this? What if that? My cycling mind will race

Desperate to get out of this headspace

I'm wrestling with my anxiety

To reach my full potential, I need to seek therapy

Empowerment

Inner Voice

Had enough, I ask

Stuck in this muck and mire, wearing the mask?

Is this my lot in life, my truth?

Constantly questioning, as if I need more proof

How did I get here?

Was it intentional, or did I accept my
circumstance out of fear?

Did I get comfortable with words unspoken?

Why did I stop caring that we were broken?

Not sure what is in store for me

But I will embrace my newfound tranquility

Your Path

Your path paved clear when you step
out on faith rather than fear

Block the naysayers and instigators
who drain your creativity

Lockstep with those who pour into your ability

Create boundaries with toxic peeps
you call family or friend

It's a decision you need not defend

Invest in taking care of self

Start first and foremost with your mental health

Find your purpose and take measured
steps with unapologetic confidence

Be leery of folks masked by false pretense

Give yourself grace when mistakes are
made in pursuit of your goal

Embrace those moments with self-affirmation
and watch your dreams unfold

Worthy

You are worthy of a love that elevates

Speaks to your spirit in a language only you can translate

A partner who spoon-feeds your soul

Nourishment in abundance should be their only goal

A relationship that reflects respect

In which spoken vows are not broken, but rather kept

A commitment that strengthens, provides inner peace

Not consumed by wondering if worrying will ever cease

You are worthy of peace of mind

Be with someone who brings joy, or be
alone—either would feel more sublime

Tired

Tired

Uninspired

Always something to do, somewhere to be

Barely time to focus on me

Rightfully called the rat race

Caught up in a competitive pace

Demands at work and home got me stressed

No time for personal interests

Bills coming at me like a tsunami

Tending to kids many needs: "Mommy, Mommy, Mommy"

Family and friends want advice and a helping hand

I'm tapped out, but they don't seem to understand

I can't be there for everybody and
leave nothing in my tank

The weight of my strong work ethic and
supportive nature, whom do I thank?

I have more years behind me than in
front, so time for a change

Sure, some will find my new behavior
uncharacteristically strange

People treat you how they see you

Time to give them a preview

Save Myself

My mind is playing tricks on me

Staring into a mirror, but my reflection I don't see

I see a woman looking depressed and dejected

Upon closer examination, I stand corrected

She is me in the realest way

No false façade on display

Showing the stress and fatigue life's struggles create

A woman trying hard with too much on her plate

Been saving people all my life

Time to save myself or continue to pay the price

Reclaiming My Time

R—Realizing I can be there for others, but not exclusively

E—Establishing boundaries in friendships
creates healthy reciprocity

C—Carving out time for self-care
is not selfish by any stretch

L—Learning to balance generosity toward others
with personal care is a form of self-respect

A—Allowing others' problems to become
my own doesn't serve me or them

I—Interceding rather than allowing friends to
decide for themselves doesn't result in a win

M—Missing time for self-reflection, so distracted
by others, results in decisions half-baked

I—Inquiring minds want to know what is at stake

N—Neglecting oneself for others is a dangerous game

G—Gleaning value solving problems other
than your own, then accept the outcome
because you only have yourself to blame

Dare Compare

You jokingly ask me to rate myself
on a scale from one to ten

Now why would I do that, my friend?

Quantify myself, as if that helps you determine my value

That's not something I need or want to do

Rating myself is unnecessary because I know my worth

There isn't a suitable scale of measurement
available on this earth

I don't compare myself to other women—
we are all uniquely divine

The fact that you don't already know
that is your problem, not mine

Just Stop

Stop chasing the coin, focus on your dreams

You're flexing for others, not living within your means

Stop sitting around talkin' about what ya gonna do

Making excuses and not seeing things through

Stop comparing yourself to others all the time

You are unique, one of a kind

Stop walking around with a chip on your
shoulder, daring someone to knock it off

Projecting a tough image out of fear
of being perceived as soft

Just stop getting in your own way

Tomorrow is not promised, so start living for today

Preparation

Preparation is crucial to success

It's about your vision, intention, the time you invest

Preparation isn't limited to the classroom

Mentors and hands-on experience also groom

Anything worth having won't come easily your way

When it feels overwhelming, keep hustling each day

Obstacles will be placed in your path as you level up in life

And failures along the way will cut like a knife

When the hard work you put in starts to manifest

Reward yourself for staying the course and doing your best

Once you arrive at a better position than
where you started on this journey

Reach back to help another become all he or she can be

Therapy

Told to push through the pain, but
that will only take you so far

It's ok to acknowledge how fragile you are

Childhood trauma tormenting and
triggering you far too long

Confront the pain, challenge it face on

Consumed by self-deprecating thoughts,
finding it hard to deal

You need a safe place to begin to heal

Don't believe that therapists manipulate your mind

You come to your own realizations over time

Speak of what consumes and holds you back

Tease out your life's fiction from fact

Put it all out there, safe from judgement
by loved ones, friends

A healing journey with a professional
means you need not pretend

You seek help for your body—why not your mind?

Your mental health is important, so to
thine own self be true and kind

Praying

Swimming in quicksand

Drowning on dry land

Running in place

Standing within empty space

Crying out as I'm held down

Screaming but there is no sound

Staring into darkness, I can clearly see

Blinding light engulfs me

Dreaming of desires unmet

Waking in a cold sweat

Worrying what tomorrow will bring

Praying, praying, praying

Her Story

You don't know her story

All you see is the fame, the glory

You don't know what it took to rise to that level

And no, she didn't make a deal with the devil

She struggled and pressed on despite many barriers

And no, she didn't have some man step in and carry her

There were days she thought her
dreams wouldn't be realized

And no, she didn't do anything shady
to see them materialize

She moved in silence gracefully,
accomplishing without brag or boast

She put the work in, more than most

Don't judge what you don't know

You don't know her story—all you see is the afterglow

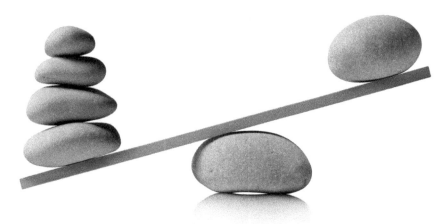

Relationships

Pick Your Face Up

Running around telling false tales
Don't bother; we all know your epic fails
Not fooling anyone, my friend
Pick your face up—start with your chin
Boasting about all you have, trying to impress
On and on about the properties in which you invest
Not fooling anyone with all the unsolicited advice and tips
Pick your face up, and don't forget those flapping lips
What you have is because of your better half
We all know it, and behind your back we laugh
Not fooling anyone, acting like you are the prize
Pick you face up, and don't forget your roaming eyes
Your identity tied up in material things; they define you
If they went away tomorrow, your identity would too
Not fooling anyone, you aren't better than your peers
Pick your face up, and don't forget those burning ears
A real shame that you place so much value on the material
The richest of us know nothing is more
valuable than bonds that are familial
Not fooling anyone, but this is the life you chose
Pick your face up, and don't forget your wooden nose

Misunderstood

Unknowingly tested the boundaries of a
friendship that spanned thirty-plus years

You gave me a reality check, and I shed too many tears

When I was holding you down, we were more than good

Once I needed the same from you, it became
a problem, so I clearly misunderstood

I misunderstood the boundaries
you placed, the limitations

I placed none and held you down during
your trials and tribulations

By your side when others came for you with tenacity

When I turned to you for support, you
said you were at your capacity

I was a sounding board, counseling you,
always in service in one way or another

Happy to do so because you were my
sister born from another mother

If someone would have told me you
would be unreliable in the end

I'd have said, "Nah, you don't know my best friend"

Clearly, I misunderstood, not in the know

So, farewell my sister friend, I have resigned to let you go

Everyone's Got One

Folks mouthing opinions, but are they
standing in their own truth?

Commenting on others' circumstances but
ignoring what's going on under their roof

Everyone's advice isn't for you, so think before you act

Not all wisdom passed on makes the intended impact

Yes, others' opinions you certainly can consider

But valuing them above your own
can make problems bigger

Look within for the answers rather than
always seeking advice from others

An outcome based on your own judgement
you can live with, you'll discover

Lover Beware

Lover beware, I'm not who I appear to be

My feelings are not real—I project
only what I want you to see

My actions are calculated and serve a purpose

My true intentions lie beneath the surface

You say you know what you feel is true

You love me, but I'm incapable of loving you

I won't lift you up or catch your fall

Listen, I'm trying to help you make the right call

You will not change me

I am resistant to romantic persuasion and heartfelt trickery

True to my nature, I will fail to meet your needs

Heed my warning, save yourself and concede

Say What

Say what you need to say

Walking around with an attitude all day

Say what's on your mind

Not playing guessing games—it's a waste of time

Say it rather than act out

Keep it civil; no need to scream or shout

Say your peace so we can talk like adults

It isn't about assigning blame; it's not about who is at fault

Say you want to come to some resolve
and lay this issue to rest

Your passive aggression makes me
shut down, I must confess

Say how much you love me and want
this relationship to succeed

Otherwise, continue to say nothing,
and I'll take my cue and leave

Not Ok

It's not ok that I get the least of you
but you expect the most of me

Although you are present, I feel your absence so deeply

It is not ok that you present your
best face for the world to see

I don't get to experience that version
of you—am I so unworthy?

Need I remind you that you signed on for this?

I wasn't standing alone at the altar
exchanging vows sealed with a kiss

We are not ok

Tell me, will the man I married
make an appearance today?

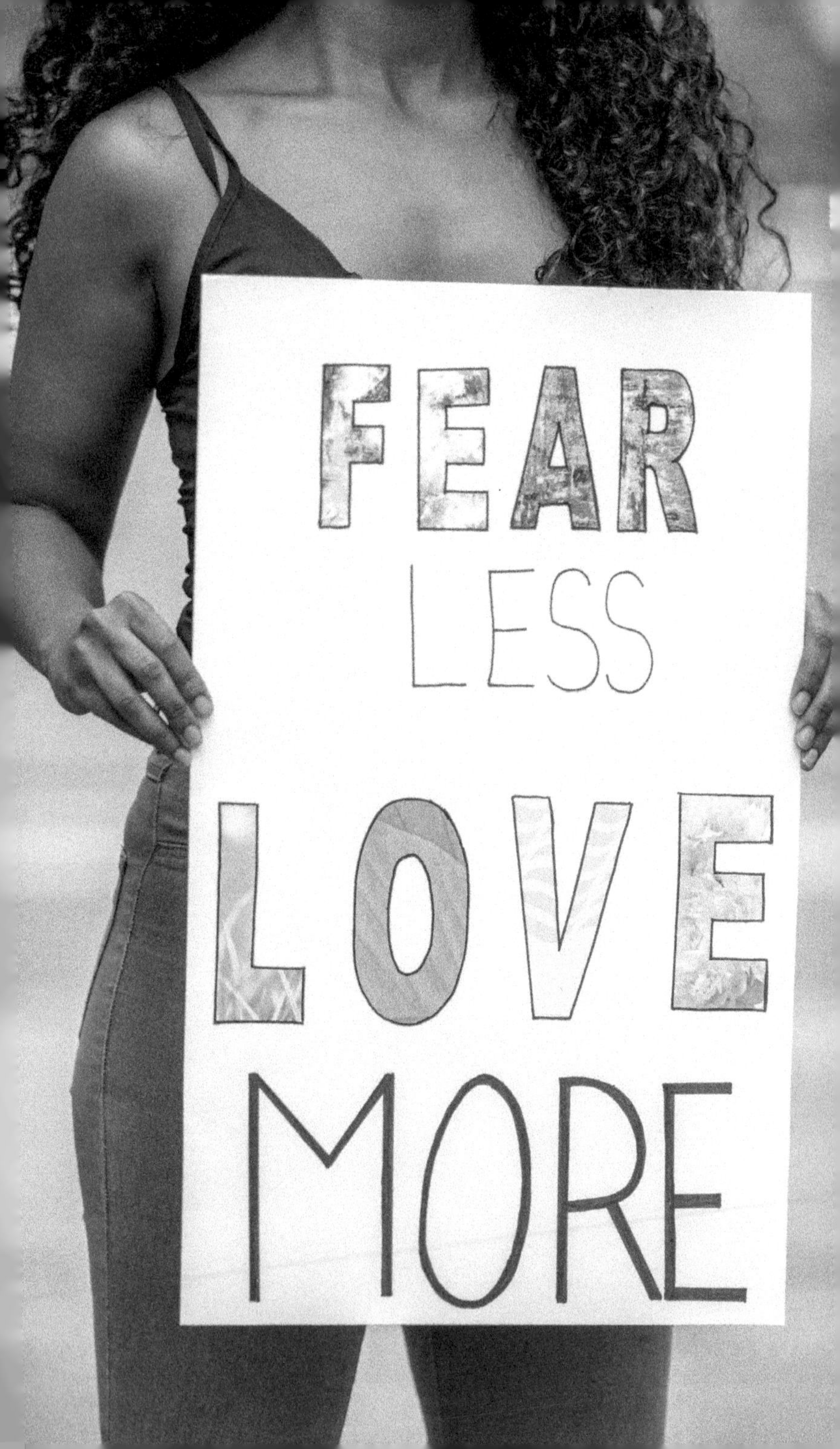
FEAR
LESS
LOVE
MORE

Society

Blood

There's blood out here in these streets

Pouring out of Black bodies whose names
have been part of too many tweets

Their crime? To exist

Stopped, held, oftentimes do not resist

Dying at the hands of police sworn to protect

Who put their knees, boots, fill in
the damn blank, on the neck

Dying at the hands of police sworn to protect

Riddling bodies with 60 bullets and
attributing blame to the suspect

There's blood out here in these streets

I hear the battle cry, "No justice, no peace"

Call upon the ancestral voices of our change-
makers who marched in protest

Channeling our anger into civil unrest

There's blood out here in these streets

Hate

Hate seethes from the entitled diminishing majority

Their menacing presence and violent
nature wielded with authority

Toxicity fills the air, so foul

Cursing the growing minority, but we won't kowtow

You aren't superior in any way

As a matter of fact, you are a cliché

Fearful of progress and being left behind

Simple-minded and prejudiced,
representing the worst of mankind

Violence is your first instinct against
those who mean you no harm

Attack upon attack, but hear the alarm

It is a new day, and that is why you are upset

But nobody is rolling over to keep you in check

Shame you can't elevate, but that's your choice

Minorities have a right to be here and have a voice

Dream

I dream of a time when I can lay my head down
not worrying about the safety of my children

Born into a world that has shown no love for them

I dream of a time when I stop feeling the gut-
wrenching fear for my children navigating
this world independent of me

For I sense danger that I fear they don't see

I dream of a time when I don't hear news of
another Black child targeted because of color

It is a never-ending story and primal
fear of every Black mother

I dream of a time when the desires of
our ancestors can be realized

If I am alive to see it, maybe then I
can finally rest my weary eyes

Change

This country has changed in ways I don't like or recognize

The truth has no value, only lies

Lies told to serve political endgames

Getting nothing done and pointing fingers
across the aisle to assign blame

Leaders fail to act on important issues that plague society

Political stalemates compromise
progress and add to my anxiety

Our political system has failed us for far too long

Party affiliation is paramount, and no
one knows right from wrong

Corrupt politicians rarely held accountable for their crimes

No standard of decency is a sign of the times

Campaign promises never realized; it is all about the win

We need a change—if not for ourselves,
think of our children

Love

Caught Feelings

Caught feelings early on

Embraced our potential back then,
and we're still going strong

Felt a closeness I'd not known before

A quiet familiarity comforting me
in ways I couldn't ignore

Never really been comfortable being vulnerable until you

Waiting for the proverbial other shoe to
drop, but it hasn't and that's new

Read romance novels about passion that escapes most

Today, those stories pale in comparison
to ours, but I dare not boast

Oh, and those late nights listening to
the quiet storm back in the day

Those sultry love songs had us feeling some kind of way

Caught feelings early on

Today, securely nestled in our love and
confident this is where I belong

Who I Am

With you my confidence heightened, no
longer frightened of showing strength

My beauty embraced despite days I
show no elegance, no grace

My talents celebrated, and I am elevated
through your unyielding praise

My vulnerability accepted without fear of
being rejected for walking in my truth

My mind eased, reminded I can't and
should not try to please everyone

My doubts quelled because you are
relentlessly compelled to lift me up

Who I am with you is enough for the both of us

True Love

Waited for you all my life

Can't adequately express how proud I am to be your wife

You stand beside me but also for me, the
embodiment of love and strength

Before you, true love was not within
reach, only at arm's length

We prioritize each other's needs, and in
doing so we are both covered

Yet know how to move independent of the
couple so neither feels smothered

Joking around and laughter are so
very much a part of our vibe

It's the deepest of connections that I describe

Shared history and a genuine friendship make us unique

Observers say our love shows in what we
exude just walking down the street

In our quiet time, I often stare, admiring my soulmate

Strong, intelligent, and handsome
with a sexy, confident gait

Yes, I watch you walk in and out of rooms and
up the stairs; you have my full attention

You got me wide open, if I failed to mention

Hypnotized by those piercing hazel
eyes when you gaze upon me

Strengthened by your hugs and assuring you in
my stillness there is nowhere I'd rather be

We don't take our love for granted and
thank God for our blessings every day

For this union was heaven sent, and
I give reverence when I pray

You

I miss your love

Not just the words and gestures, but that sensual,
physical love that permeates and subdues me

It's all I can think of…

Your lips, as they carefully caress the delicate
skin that brings forth erotic pleasure

The way you make my legs quiver, my
heart race…beyond measure

Your touch

The way you gently stroke my skin with your fingertips,
tantalizing and daring me not to respond…much

The weight of your body upon mine

I feel your strength and vulnerability at the same time

I miss our love when it's just us doing
what we do, how we do

In other words, I miss you

Out of Reach

My mind is distracted with thoughts of you

But you are not within reach, totally out of view

My dreams are vivid reminders of our bond

When I awake, reach out, I'm reminded you're gone

My photos depict the happiest of times spent

This humble heart cherishes the memories
and what they represent

My conversations about you and
what we had provoke a smile

For I long to be in your presence once more, my
heavenly love, but I feel it may be a while

Milton Keynes UK
Ingram Content Group UK Ltd.
UKHW021140010424
440413UK00008B/145

9 798822 941847